For Dylan and Kara Wertham

—Judy

Text Copyright © 2015 Judy Young
Illustration Copyright © 2015 Michael Glenn Monroe

Sleeping Bear Press
2395 South Huron Parkway, Suite 200
Ann Arbor, MI 48104
www.sleepingbearpress.com

Printed and bound in the United States.

10 9 8 7 6 5 4 3 2 1

Library of Congress Cataloging-in-Publication Data.

Young, Judy, 1956- author.
Sleepy snoozy cozy coozy : a book of animal beds /
written by Judy Young ; illustrated by Michael Glenn Monroe.
pages cm
Audience: 4-8.
ISBN 978-1-58536-908-9
1. Animals—Habitations—North America—Juvenile literature.
2. Nursery rhymes. I. Monroe, Michael Glenn, illustrator. II. Title.
QL756.Y68 2015
590—dc23

Sleepy Snoozy Cozy Coozy: A Book of Animal Beds is a
collection of poems with accompanying nonfiction text about
where and how certain North American animals, including
moles, moose, beavers, build their beds and go to sleep.

Sleepy Snoozy Cozy Coozy

A Book of Animal Beds

Written by **Judy Young** and Illustrated by **Michael Glenn Monroe**

In the branches of a tree
An eagle sits so worry-free.
He shuts his eyes to get some rest
All comfy in his great big nest.

A sticky twiggy
Very biggy
Round and scratchy
Feathery patchy

Picky pokey
Piney oaky
Place where you won't lay your head
But to an eagle it's a bed.

....

Eagles build the biggest nests of all birds. Up to ten
feet wide and weighing several tons, these nests are
like huge platforms made of sticks with a soft layer of
moss, leaves, and grasses on top. Eagles return to the
same nest each summer, year after year. They live on it
until their babies fly away.

Eagles have three eyelids. They close two when they sleep.
The third is used to clean their eyes when they blink.
How many eyelids do you close when you sleep?

Way down deep, deep in the ground
In tunnels winding all around
Softly sleeps a little mole
Curled up snuggly in his hole.

A dirty yucky
Muckalucky
Dark and dreary
Not too cheery

Tight and crampy
Needs a lampy
Place where you won't lay your head
But to a mole it is a bed.

Moles live in underground tunnels where they find
worms, larvae, and insects to eat. Digging up to 60
feet a day, they loosen the dirt with their thick claws.
Then they use their strong, shovel-like feet to push the
dirt from the tunnel into a mound around the tunnel's
entrance. They dig a special nesting chamber,
lined with fine grasses, to raise their young.

Moles dig and eat for about four
hours, then sleep for another four.
How long do you sleep?

In tall grasses of a glade
A spider weaves from blade to blade
Up and down and flow and ebb
Until he climbs onto his web.

A springy stringy
Oh so clingy
Frail and flossy
Quite criss-crossy

Sticky tacky
Stay way backy
Place where you won't lay your head
But to a spider it's a bed.

....

Many spiders build webs using strong, silk threads
made by special glands, called spinnerets, located at
the tip of the spider's abdomen. Some threads are
sticky, others are not. The spider sits on its web and
waits. When an insect gets caught on a sticky thread,
the web vibrates and the spider runs along the
nonsticky threads to get its meal.

It's not known if spiders sleep every day, but some
hibernate in winter with their legs pulled in close to their
bodies. Do you curl up to sleep, too?

In a stream where water gushes
Scooting backward a crayfish rushes
To a spot it calls its own
Way beneath a rocky stone.

A wet and drippy
Cold and nippy
Stony zoney
All aloney

Crushing cramming
Watery slamming
Place where you won't lay your head
But to a crayfish it's a bed.

Crayfish (also called crawfish or crawdads) live in streams, rivers, lakes, and ponds. They walk forward, eating vegetation, worms, insects, and snails, crushing and tearing their food with their pincer claws. When threatened, they quickly scoot backward, finding shelter under a nearby rock or in a muddy burrow.

A crayfish sleeps during the day, often on its side, holding onto a rock or the mud with one of its ten legs. Do you sleep on your side?

Near the banks of a river
Through a hole, just a sliver
A beaver dives and then he kicks
Into his lodge of logs and sticks.

A limb and loggy
Dim and soggy
Crusty cruddy
Dried up muddy

Leafy willowy
Not too pillowy
Place where you won't lay your head
But to a beaver it's a bed.

Beavers use sticks, rocks, and mud to build lodges by
the banks of streams and rivers or in the middle of ponds
or lakes. To enter the lodge, beavers dive underwater and
swim into a tunnel that leads upward to two chambers above
the water's surface. One chamber is where the beaver dries off.
The other is where it sleeps, eats, and raises its young.

Beavers are nocturnal, sleeping during the day on beds
of grasses and leafy twigs, which they can eat later.
Can you eat your bed?

In a cavern underground
From the ceiling upside down
Clinging with his feet so tight
Is where a bat will spend the night.

A cold and clammy
Bit toe jammy
Dark and spacious
Quite curvaceous

Drafty airy
Dank and scary
Place where you won't lay your head
But to a bat it is a bed.

....

Bats are the only mammals that can truly fly. They sleep
hanging upside down, holding onto the ceilings of caves, rock
ledges, tree limbs, and even in attics and barns. Their wings
are not strong enough to lift themselves in flight, so when
they want to fly, they simply let go, and drop into flight.

Bats are nocturnal, sleeping during the day with
their wings wrapped around their bodies.
What do you wrap around you when you sleep?

In among the cypress trees
Blending in so no one sees
A 'gator looking like a log
Snoozes near a swampy bog.

A hot and buggy
Mossy muggy
Sleazy slimey
All the timey

Lakey snakey
Stay awakey
Place where you won't lay your head
But to a 'gator it's a bed.

Alligators dig out "'gator holes," long water-filled hollows in the mud, where they will stay in extreme hot or cold weather. They sleep during the day, basking in the sun with their eyes closed. Often, their mouths are wide open, which helps them stay cool.

Alligators do not sleep while floating. They may look like they're asleep floating in the water, but they are awake, and can quickly go after unsuspecting prey.
Do you ever pretend to be asleep?

Near the ocean, near the sea
Where waves crash and tumble free
A hermit crab does very well
Sleeping in a borrowed shell.

A spindly spiny
Way too tiny
Sandy gritty
Itty bitty

Tight and tomb-y
Not too roomy
Place where you won't lay your head
But to this crab it is a bed.

A hermit crab cannot grow its own shell. To protect its soft abdomen from predators, the hermit crab uses empty shells made by other creatures, mostly sea snails. It climbs in backward, with its claws near the shell's opening, and carries this borrowed home around with it until it grows out of it. Then it finds a bigger shell for its home.

Hermit crabs are nocturnal, sleeping during the day in their borrowed shells. Do you ever borrow a bed to sleep in?

In the forest thick with trees
A moose will bend his wobbly knees.
Laying down he starts to snore
Sleeping on the forest floor.

A dark and freaky
Sometimes leaky
Dirty beetle-y
Pinecone needle-y

Brushy bushy
Not too cushy
Place where you won't lay your head
But to a moose it is a bed.

....

Moose make their homes in the open tundra, boggy
wetlands, mountain meadows, and deep forests of the
northern parts of the United States and Canada. A single
moose's home range may cover up to 25 square miles.
When a moose gets tired, it lays down to sleep wherever it
happens to be.

Moose sleep at night but wake up early, before dawn, and
go to bed late, after dusk. Do you wake up before dawn?
Do you go to bed after dusk?

In the desert hot and dry
Where the sun glares from the sky
The little kit fox likes to stay
In his den, asleep all day.

A hidden hollow
Slim and small-o
Dark as nighty
Out of sighty

Scruffy scrubby
Little cubby
Place where you won't lay your head
But to this fox it is a bed.

Living in the deserts of the southwestern United States
and northern Mexico, the kit fox is nocturnal, avoiding
the desert heat by sleeping in dens during the day. It may
dig dens in the sandy soil, take over dens made by other
animals, or even sleep in man-made structures such as
drainage pipes.

The smallest fox in North America, the kit fox moves
from den to den. It may sleep in up to 24 different
dens a year. How many places do you sleep in?

In the ocean far and wide
Swimming, diving, through the tide
A world so wet, so dark and deep
That's where a dolphin goes to sleep.

A black and bluey
See right throughy
Swooshy swishy
Full of fishy

Salty foamy
Watery homey
Place where you won't lay your head
But to a dolphin it's a bed.

....

Dolphins are mammals and must go above the water's surface to breathe. But, unlike most mammals, dolphins must think about when to take a breath, and they can't think about breathing if they are totally asleep. So, only half of a dolphin's brain goes to sleep and only one eye closes at a time. The other half stays awake to think about breathing. After about two hours, one side wakes up and the other side goes to sleep.

Do you have to think about breathing when you sleep?

In a room that's in a home
On a mattress soft as foam
A little child curls up to sleep
Underneath the blankets deep.

A silky puffy
Toasty fluffy
Comfy dreamy
Warm moonbeamy

Sleepy snoozy
Cozy coozy
Place where you might lay your head
For you're a child and it's your bed.

Children live in many different types of homes. Most children
live in houses, house trailers, or apartment buildings. Some
children may live in a hotel, a tent, a lean-to, or even on a boat.
What kind of home do you live in?

Children usually sleep at night but may take a nap during the day, too.
Most children sleep on a bed, but some sleep in a crib, on a cot or a
couch, in a hammock, or on a mat. What do you sleep on?